TIMELINES

The Civil Rights Movement

Colin Hynson

ARCTURUS

This edition first published in 2010 by Arcturus Publishing
Distributed by Black Rabbit Books
P.O. Box 3263
Mankato
Minnesota MN 56002

Copyright © 2010 Arcturus Publishing Limited

Printed in China

Library of Congress Cataloging-in-Publication Data

Hynson, Colin.
  The civil rights movement / Colin Hynson.
     p. cm. -- (Timelines)
  Includes index.
  ISBN 978-1-84837-638-0 (library bound)
  1. African Americans--Civil rights--History--20th century--Juvenile literature. 2.
Civil rights movements--United States--History--20th century--Juvenile literature.
3. United States--Race relations--Juvenile literature. I. Title.
  E185.61.H996 2011
  323.1196'073--dc22
                      2009051261

Series concept: Alex Woolf
Editor and picture researcher: Carron Brown
Consultant: James Vaughan
Designer: Ariadne Ward

Picture credits:
Corbis: cover (Bettmann), 5, 6 (Bettmann), 7 (Bettmann), 10 (Bettmann), 11 (Bettmann), 14
(Bettmann), 15 (Bettmann), 16 (Jack Moebus), 17 (Bettmann), 18 (Bettmann), 19 (Bettmann), 20
(Bettmann), 21 (Bettmann), 22 (Bettmann), 23 (Bob Adelman), 24 (Bettmann), 25 (Bettmann), 26
(Steve Schapiro), 27 (Bettmann), 28 (Bettmann), 29, 31 (Bettmann), 32 (Bettmann), 33 (Bettmann),
34 (Bettmann), 35 (Bob Adelman), 41 (Bettmann), 43 (Peter Turnley), 45 (Ralf-Finn Hestoft).
Getty Images: 4, 36 (Bentley Archive/Popperfoto), 37 (John Dominis/Time & Life Pictures),
38 (Joseph Louw/Time Life Pictures), 44 (Charles Ommanney).
Rex Features: 12 (Courtesy Everett Collection), 13 (Courtesy Everett Collection), 39 (CSU
Archives/Everett Collection), 42.
Topfoto: 8 (The Granger Collection), 9 (The Granger Collection), 30 (AP), 40 (Topham/AP).

Cover picture: Martin Luther King, Jr., speaks to a crowd of thousands during the
civil rights march to the Washington Memorial on August 28, 1963.

ISBN: 978-1-84837-638-0
SL001322US
Supplier 03, Date 0210

Contents

The First Civil Rights Act

APRIL 19, 1866

On April 19, 1866, the US Congress passed the first-ever Civil Rights Act. It gave black Americans the right to own their own property, to have legal protection in business, and to take people to court. The act was also the first time that black Americans were called citizens of the United States. This meant that black Americans would have the same rights and privileges as all other US citizens.

This Harper's Weekly *magazine cover from November 16, 1867 shows black Americans voting for the first time. This was a landmark event for civil rights.*

THE END OF THE CIVIL WAR

Since 1861, the United States had been torn apart by a war between the Southern and Northern halves of the country. There were many reasons for the war, but it was the issue of slavery that divided the country. Abraham Lincoln had been elected president on a promise to stop the growth of slavery, but 11 states in the South declared their secession from the United States, and war soon began. It did not end until 1865, with the defeat of the South, and 4 million black people were freed from slavery.

AFTER THE CIVIL WAR

A few months before the American Civil War ended, Congress passed the 13th Amendment to the Constitution, which officially abolished slavery throughout the country. It was closely followed by the 14th Amendment, which made everybody an equal

Equal rights

"All persons within the jurisdiction of the United States shall have the same right in every State and Territory to make and enforce contracts, to sue, be parties, give evidence, and to the full and equal benefit of all laws and proceedings for the security of persons and property as is enjoyed by white citizens, and shall be subject to like punishment, pains, penalties, taxes, licenses, and exactions of every kind, and to no other."

Excerpt from the Civil Rights Act, 1866.

citizen before the law, and the 15th Amendment, which gave every US citizen the right to vote. The 14th Amendment was intended to give full rights to all former slaves. However, many of the Southern states did not support these amendments and also found ways to ignore the 1866 Civil Rights Act. In January 1875, the Supreme Court ruled that the 14th and 15th Amendments only applied to facilities provided by the states and could not be used to make racial discrimination illegal between individuals and organizations.

THE 1875 ACT

Another Civil Rights Act was passed in 1875. This act made it illegal to discriminate on the basis of race in public places, such as restaurants. In 1883, the Supreme Court ruled that the 1875 act was unconstitutional on the basis that businesses had the right to choose which customers they served and which they could ignore. This allowed businesses that provided public facilities to choose to exclude black people.

CROSS-REFERENCE THE CIVIL RIGHTS ACT, 1964: PAGES 28–29

Hiram Rhodes Revels was the first black member of the US Senate. In his maiden speech on March 16, 1870, he urged senators to think well of black Americans. He worked continuously for black equality during the year of his term.

Plessy v. Ferguson

On May 6, 1896, the Supreme Court passed a resolution stating that it was not unconstitutional to provide separate facilities for black and white people as long as the facilities were the same for both groups. This decision formed the basis for widespread discrimination and segregation throughout the Southern states of the country for many years to come.

JIM CROW LAWS

In the years after the Civil War, the states of the South passed a number of laws that made it legal to separate black and white people when they used public facilities such as schools, restaurants or public transportation. These laws were known as "Jim Crow" laws. For example, in North Carolina, black and white people were allocated separate tables in libraries, and many courts even provided separate Bibles for black and white people for swearing in witnesses.

RESTRICTING THE VOTE

Among the most infamous examples of Jim Crow laws were attempts by Southern states to deny black citizens the vote. Some states passed "grandfather clauses" that took away voting rights from people who were not citizens before 1866. This effectively meant all freed slaves. There were also laws passed that gave the vote only to people who paid certain taxes, called "poll taxes", or

who passed a literacy test. This meant that many black people had the right to vote taken away from them since they were too poor to pay the poll tax and literacy levels among black Americans were much lower than among their white counterparts.

Water fountains were only one of the many services segregated across the Southern states with separate facilities for white people and black people.

An example of a Jim Crow law

"It shall be unlawful for any amateur white baseball team to play baseball on any vacant lot or baseball diamond within two blocks of a playground devoted to the Negro race, and it shall be unlawful for any amateur colored baseball team to play baseball in any vacant lot or baseball diamond within two blocks of any playground devoted to the white race."

Law passed by the state of Georgia in the 1880s.

1850s ▶ The character of Jim Crow is a common act in minstrel shows.

July 10, 1890 ▶ The state of Louisiana passes the Separate Car Act, which creates separate train cars for white and black passengers.

June 7, 1892 ▶ Homer A. Plessy is arrested for sitting in a train car reserved for white passengers only.

May 6, 1896 ▶ The Supreme Court passes a resolution stating that providing separate facilities for black and white people is not unconstitutional.

1910 ▶ Every state in the former Confederacy has laws that segregate public places.

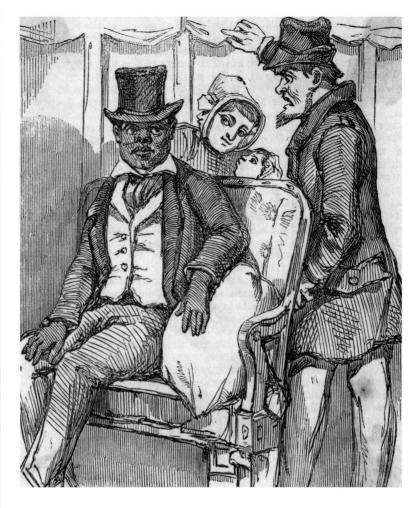

This contemporary illustration shows a black American being asked to leave a whites-only train carriage.

"SEPARATE BUT EQUAL"

In 1892, Homer A. Plessy was arrested for riding on a train in Louisiana in a car that was reserved for white passengers only. Using the 14th Amendment, Plessy claimed that the Louisiana law that allowed separate carriages for black and white people was unconstitutional. A local judge, John H. Ferguson, ruled that the law was legal under the Constitution. Plessy then took his case to the Supreme Court. All but one of the judges on the Supreme Court agreed that as long as the law gave equal treatment to both black and white passengers, then it was constitutional to provide separate facilities.

CROSS-REFERENCE SEGREGATION ON TRANSPORTATION: PAGES 12–13, 18–19

The NAACP Is Formed

On June 1, 1909, the National Association for the Advancement of Colored People (NAACP) was formed. It became the most important civil rights organization fighting for the rights of black people in the United States. It is still active today and has a membership of about half a million.

THE NIAGARA MOVEMENT

In 1905, a group of 30 prominent black Americans met to discuss the problems that were facing the black population of the United States and to look for possible solutions. Since many hotels in the country were segregated, they decided to meet in a hotel on the Canadian side of Niagara Falls. As a result, the group, led by academic William DuBois, became known as the Niagara Movement. However, it remained a small group, and it soon struggled to survive. One of the reasons for this was that at the time, black educator Booker T. Washington was urging black Americans to forget about calling for equal rights and to concentrate instead on advancing themselves through hard work. These beliefs were popular among many black leaders. However, DuBois believed that equal rights could only be achieved through changing the law.

MEETING IN 1909

The Niagara Movement decided that it needed to become a larger group if it was to survive. In 1909, about 60 black and white citizens who agreed to fight for equal rights for all in the United States met in New York City and the NAACP was formed. The first president of the NAACP was a white lawyer from Boston, Moorfield Storey. For the first few years, many of the most important members of the NAACP were white, and DuBois was the only black American on the first board of the NAACP.

NAACP ACHIEVEMENTS

For the first 30 years of its existence, the NAACP concentrated on fighting the Jim Crow laws (particularly those that took away the right to vote) and discrimination in employment. They also worked hard to get anti-lynching laws passed. Since World War II, the NAACP has played a major part in the struggle against segregation and in fighting racial discrimination in many areas

JUNE 1, 1909

A lynching banner erected by the National Association for the Advancement of Colored People in New York. Each time a black American was killed by a lynching mob, the banner was hung from the NAACP office.

| TIMELINE | THE NAACP, 1905–1946 |

TIMELINE

THE NAACP, 1905–1946

1905 ▶ A group of 30 black Americans meets at Niagara Falls.

August 14, 1908 ▶ The Springfield Race Riot in Springfield, Illinois, highlights a need for a civil rights organization.

1909 ▶ The NAACP is founded.

1914 ▶ The NAACP has 6,000 members and wins the right for black Americans to serve as officers in World War I.

September 30, 1919 ▶ The Elaine Race Riot occurs in Arkansas, which results in over 200 black Americans being killed by white vigilantes and troops. The NAACP gives legal support to accused black Americans.

1946 ▶ The NAACP has around 600,000 members.

of American life such as housing and education. It also works with black Americans in prison and in military service.

NAACP youth and student members protesting against segregation laws in 1947.

Speech by a civil rights leader of the NAACP

"The object of the National Association is to create an organization which will endeavour to smooth the path of the Negro race upward, and create a public opinion which will frown upon discrimination against their property rights ... We want to make race prejudice as unfashionable as it is now fashionable."

Moorfield Storey, the first president of the NAACP, speaks about the organization in 1910.

CROSS-REFERENCE
THE NAACP:
PAGES 10–11, 17, 24

Segregation Is Over

Thurgood Marshall (middle) with lawyers George Hayes (left) and James Nabrit (right) in front of the Supreme Court building. They won their case in court against segregation.

On May 17, 1954, the Supreme Court passed a judgement that changed the course of civil rights in the United States. In the case of *Brown v. the Board of Education*, the judges on the Supreme Court declared that racial segregation in education was unconstitutional and therefore against the law. This decision overturned the *Plessy v. Ferguson* case of 1896.

LINDA BROWN

The case of *Brown v. the Board of Education* began in 1951, when, with the help of the NAACP, a group of black parents in Topeka, Kansas, asked for their children to go to local white schools. One of the parents, Oliver Brown, wanted his daughter, Linda, to go to a white school that was closer to their home. He was supported by Robert Carter, a lawyer working for the NAACP. The local court in Kansas found that segregation in local schools was legal as long as black and white schools gave an equally good education. The NAACP decided to take the case to the Supreme Court.

THE SUPREME COURT DECISION

In June 1952, the Supreme Court agreed to hear the case of *Brown v. the Board of Education*. The case for the Browns was argued by Thurgood Marshall, the top NAACP lawyer. He had taken 15 other cases to the Supreme Court, winning 13 of them, but this was the most important case

The doll study

In the 1940s, two psychologists studied children ages six to nine years old. When asked about black- and white-skinned dolls, black children thought more highly of the white dolls than of the black dolls. The study concluded that experiencing an inferior status in society was psychologically damaging. This supported the legal team in *Brown v. the Board of Education*.

TIMELINE

BROWN v. THE BOARD OF EDUCATION, 1951–1954

1951 ▶ A group of black parents in Topeka, Kansas, ask the NAACP to help them find places for their children in white schools. After a local court states that segregation in local schools is legal, the NAACP takes the case to the Supreme Court.

June 1952 ▶ The Supreme Court agrees to hear the case of *Brown v. the Board of Education*.

May 17, 1954 ▶ The Supreme Court delivers a verdict that states that black and white children should not be segregated in public schools.

that he had ever argued before the court. He attacked the belief in a separate but equal system of education by saying that segregation in schools made black students feel inferior, which meant that they were not able to learn as well as white students.

Shortly after noon on Monday, May 17, 1954, the Supreme Court delivered its opinion on the case. Earl Warren, the chief justice on the Supreme Court, read it out to a packed courtroom. The judges on the Supreme Court had unanimously decided that separate schools for black and white children could not be equal and violated the rights of black children under the 14th Amendment. The NAACP held a victory celebration, and many newspapers in the North supported the Supreme Court decision. In the South, however, there was opposition to the ruling. They felt that the Supreme Court did not have the right to tell individual states how to run their school systems.

CROSS-REFERENCE SEGREGATION IN SCHOOLS: PAGES 14–15

On May 17, 1954, a mother and daughter were photographed on the steps of the Supreme Court after the high court's ruling in the Brown v. Board of Education *case. The newspaper's headline states that the Supreme Court has banned segregation in schools.*

Rosa Parks and the Montgomery Bus Boycott

DECEMBER 1, 1955

On December 1, 1955, Rosa Parks boarded a bus in Montgomery, Alabama. The buses in the city were segregated, and Rosa Parks sat in a row of seats that was designated for white people. She was told to move, but she refused. Parks was arrested, and this sparked the first mass protest in the civil rights movement.

SEGREGATION ON THE BUSES

By law, the front seats on Montgomery buses were reserved for white people. Black passengers had to sit in the back seats. The middle seats could be used by black people, but if a white person had to stand, then any black passenger sitting in the middle had to give up his or her seat, even if he or she had to stand. This is what happened to Rosa Parks. The driver asked all the black people on a row of seats to move so that one white person could have a seat. They all moved except for Parks.

THE BUS BOYCOTT

Parks allowed local black leaders to use her case to start a boycott of the buses of Montgomery. They formed an organization called the Montgomery Improvement Association, and a young minister named Martin Luther King, Jr., was selected to be the president of

the association. From December 5, 1955 until December 20, 1956, thousands of black people refused to use the segregated buses. By the end of January 1956, the boycott was beginning to have an effect. Shopkeepers reported that they were losing a lot of money because people were not using the buses. The bus company was losing a lot of money and had to raise fares. The city authorities reacted by arresting the leaders, including Martin Luther King, Jr. Their appearance in court was widely reported in newspapers and radio and television stations across the country and turned the boycott into national news.

THE BOYCOTT ENDS

On June 4, 1956, a local court in Alabama ruled on a case brought to

Rosa Parks had her fingerprints taken at the police station after her arrest. Four days later, she was convicted of disorderly conduct for refusing to obey the segregation laws.

TIMELINE

THE MONTGOMERY BUS BOYCOTT, 1955–1956

December 1, 1955
▶ Rosa Parks is arrested for refusing to move from the white section of a bus, sparking the first mass protests of the civil rights movement.

December 5, 1955– December 20, 1956
▶ Thousands of black people in Montgomery refuse to use the segregated buses.

June 4, 1956
▶ A local court in Alabama rules that segregation violates the 14th Amendment.

December 21, 1956
▶ Martin Luther King, Jr., boards the first-ever integrated bus in Montgomery.

it by four Montgomery black women asking for the end of segregation on buses. The judges ruled in favor of the women and said that segregation violated the 14th Amendment. Officials in Montgomery took the case to the Supreme Court. The Supreme Court supported the decision of the local court and declared that laws requiring segregation on buses were unconstitutional. On December 21, 1956, Martin Luther King, Jr., and other black leaders boarded the first-ever integrated bus in Montgomery.

CROSS-REFERENCE SEGREGATION ON TRANSPORTATION: PAGES 6–7, 18–19

Martin Luther King, Jr. (center left), on the first integrated Montgomery bus.

The arrest

"A few minutes later, two policemen got on the bus, and they approached me and asked if the driver had asked me to stand up, and I said yes, and they wanted to know why I hadn't. I said I didn't think I should have to stand up ... They placed me under arrest then and had me get in a police car."

Excerpt from an interview with Rosa Parks in *My Soul Is Rested: Movement Days in the Deep South Remembered*, by Howell Raines (Penguin, 1983).

Crisis at Little Rock

On September 4, 1957, nine black students tried to enter all-white Central High School in Little Rock, Arkansas. However, the governor of Arkansas, Orval Faubus, sent in local troops to stop them from getting into the school. President Eisenhower had to send in army troops to make sure that the students could attend the school.

THE CRISIS BEGINS

Little Rock seemed an unlikely place for a battle over racial segregation. All of the libraries, parks, and buses were integrated. Only five days after the *Brown v. the Board of Education* decision was made, schools in Little Rock, including Central High, began to plan for full integration. However, Governor Faubus was opposed to integration in Arkansas's schools and tried to prevent the nine students from attending Central High. On September 3, he sent 250 local troops to the school to stop them from entering. The students decided not to try to enter the school.

The next day, they did try to go to school, but their way was blocked by troops. There was also a large crowd of white people who did not want white schools to accept black students. As the nine students approached, the crowd shouted threats and abuse at them.

EISENHOWER INTERVENES

President Eisenhower was under pressure to intervene and ensure that all schools fell in line with the decision

Elizabeth Eckford ignored the hostile screams and stares of fellow students on her first day at Central High School. She and eight fellow black students bravely faced the angry crowds but were turned back when troops blocked their way.

Mob rule

"They moved closer and closer. Somebody started yelling, 'Lynch her! Lynch her!' I tried to see a friendly face somewhere in the mob—someone who maybe would help. I looked into the face of an old woman and it seemed a kind face, but when I looked at her again, she spat on me."
Interview with Elizabeth Eckford in *The Long Shadow of Little Rock*, by Daisy Bates (University of Arkansas Press, 1987).

TIMELINE

CENTRAL HIGH SCHOOL STUDENTS, 1954–1958

May 17, 1954 ▶ The Supreme Court rules that public schools should be desegregated.

September 3, 1957 ▶ The governor of Arkansas sends 250 troops to Central High School, Little Rock, to stop black students from entering.

September 4, 1957 ▶ Nine black students try to enter Central High School in Little Rock and are blocked by troops.

September 23, 1957 ▶ Over 1,000 white protestors force the black students from the school.

September, 24 1957 ▶ President Eisenhower sends 1,000 army troops to protect the students.

May 27, 1958 ▶ Ernest Green becomes the first black person to graduate from Central High School.

of *Brown v. the Board of Education.* He told Governor Faubus that the troops should be used only to ensure the safety of the nine students. Faubus responded by withdrawing the troops from the school on September 23. Over 1,000 white protestors surrounded the school and forced the students out of the building.

On September 24, the president sent over 1,000 army troops to protect the students as they went to school. They ringed the building with bayonets fixed to their rifles and stood guard as the nine black students entered and left the school. After two months, they were replaced by local troops. Throughout the rest of the year, white protestors continued to shout abuse and threaten the students. On May 27, 1958, Ernest Green became the first black person to graduate from Central High. However, in September 1958, Governor Faubus ordered all high schools in Little Rock to close to try to block integration. After a year of lost education, the federal courts ordered the schools to reopen in 1959.

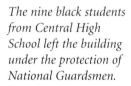

CROSS-REFERENCE SEGREGATION IN SCHOOLS: PAGES 10–11

The nine black students from Central High School left the building under the protection of National Guardsmen.

Peaceful Sit-ins

FEBRUARY 1, 1960

During the first sit-in at Greensboro, four people sat at a whites-only lunch counter at Woolworth's.

On February 1, 1960, four black students in Greensboro, North Carolina, walked into their local Woolworth's. They bought some school supplies and then sat down at the lunch counter. The seats that they chose were reserved for white customers. The waitress refused to serve them so, the students remained seated until the store closed.

THE SIT-INS SPREAD

The next day, the four students returned to the Woolworth's lunch counter, this time with 20 other students. They simply sat down and the counter staff ignored them. On the third day of the occupation, more students arrived and took over 63 of the 66 seats. The Greensboro sit-in then spread to other segregated lunch counters in town.

Within two weeks, sit-ins were taking place in South Carolina and Virginia. In two months, the student sit-in movement had spread to over 50 towns and cities in nine states. As the sit-ins spread, there was a strong reaction from some white hecklers. Students had ketchup and salt poured over their heads. In Nashville, the students were attacked and pulled off their seats. Yet the students did not fight back and continued with their non-violent actions.

THE SNCC IS FOUNDED

On Easter 1960, a group of students from black colleges gathered together in Raleigh, North Carolina. They met to discuss the sit-ins and to plan future tactics. One of the main speakers at this meeting was 55-year-old Ella Baker. She urged the young students to continue in order to inspire others to join in. The meeting concluded with the formation of the Student Nonviolent Coordinating Committee (SNCC), which was pronounced "snick." The SNCC began to coordinate the sit-in protests. Many of the sit-in protestors, including Martin Luther King, Jr., were arrested. None of the white people who attacked the protestors were arrested.

THE SUCCESS OF THE SIT-INS

By the end of 1960, over 70,000 people had taken part in peaceful sit-ins and other protests around the country. In that time, the lunch counter at the Woolworth's in Greensboro had become fully integrated and black people could sit anywhere they liked. On May 10, several lunch counters in Nashville opened to black customers. By the end of the year, hundreds of stores and restaurants throughout the South were no longer segregated. The peaceful sit-in movement had been a complete success.

CROSS-REFERENCE
THE SNCC: PAGES
18–19, 32–33,
36–37

Segregation protesters at a sit-in at a lunch counter in Jackson, Mississippi, after being sprayed with sauce and beaten on the back and head by the crowd.

The importance of the sit-ins

The sit-ins marked a change in the civil rights movement since they were mostly led by young people and took place in public, not in courtrooms. The sit-ins showed that non-violence could be a useful action toward desegregation.

The Freedom Rides

MAY 4, 1961

On May 4, 1961, 13 volunteers (seven black and six white people) boarded two buses in Washington, DC. Their intention was to ride to Alabama and Louisiana and to challenge segregation not only on buses, but also in bus terminals and stations. All of the volunteers had pledged that they would rather go to jail than give up their campaign.

THE FREEDOM RIDES IN ALABAMA

On May 14, one bus arrived in Anniston, Alabama, where it was attacked by a mob of about 200 people, who smashed the windows and slashed the tires. The bus got away, but with the mob chasing it. About 6 miles (10 kilometers) outside the town, the bus tires went flat and the bus had to stop, where it was attacked again. This time, a firebomb was thrown into the bus. Luckily, everyone left the vehicle before it burst into flames. A photograph of the burnt-out bus was shown around the world.

The other bus drove to Birmingham, Alabama. A group of 30 men, all members of the Ku Klux Klan, were waiting for it with baseball bats and bicycle chains. The Freedom Riders were badly beaten. Throughout the attack, there was no sign of any police officers. As a result of these attacks, the drivers on both buses refused to continue and the Freedom Rides were abandoned.

THE SNCC TAKES OVER

The first Freedom Rides were organized by the Congress for Racial Equality (CORE). However, it was the SNCC that decided to continue with the Freedom Rides, and a bus was sent to Birmingham and then on to Montgomery, Alabama. John Patterson, the governor of Alabama, promised the federal government that he would protect the Freedom Riders, and there was a police escort between Birmingham and Montgomery. However, when the

This is the famous photograph of a fireman spraying water on the burning shell of a Greyhound bus after it was attacked by a mob.

Freedom song

**"I'm taking a ride on the Greyhound bus line.
I'm riding the front seat to Jackson this time.
Hallelujah, I'm traveling;
Hallelujah, ain't it fine?
Hallelujah, I'm traveling
Down Freedom's main line"**

Song sung by Freedom Riders on the route from Alabama to Mississippi, May 1961.

THE DESEGREGATION OF BUSES, 1961

May 4, 1961 ▶ Volunteers board two buses in Washington, DC, to campaign for an end to segregation.

May, 14 1961 ▶ One bus arrives in Anniston, Alabama, and is attacked by a mob of 200 people.

May, 14 1961 ▶ The second bus arrives in Birmingham, Alabama, and is attacked by 30 Ku Klux Klan members.

May 17, 1961 ▶ The SNCC continues with the Freedom Rides.

May 20, 1961 ▶ Local troops are sent to Montgomery to protect the Freedom Riders, 12 of whom are arrested for using a whites-only toilet.

November 1, 1961 ▶ The federal government issues an order that bus terminals and buses have to be desegregated.

bus approached Montgomery, the police cars drove away. A mob attacked the bus and beat the volunteers on board.

BUS SEGREGATION ENDS

The federal government realized that Governor Patterson had broken his promise and could not be trusted again. Local troops were sent to Montgomery to protect the Freedom Riders as they drove on to Mississippi. At the bus terminal in Jackson, Mississippi, 12 volunteers tried to use the whites-only toilet and were arrested. More Freedom Riders arrived in Jackson and were also arrested. Finally, the federal government acted. On November 1, 1961, an order was issued that prohibited segregated buses from crossing state lines. The bus terminals that served these buses were also desegregated.

CROSS-REFERENCE SEGREGATION ON TRANSPORTATION: PAGES 6–7, 12–13

As the bus carrying Freedom Riders arrived in Jackson, Mississippi, police officers with dogs prepared to arrest and jail those on board.

The Albany Movement

NOVEMBER 17, 1961

On November 17, 1961, a group of local civil rights organizations met in Albany, Georgia. They formed the Albany Movement in order to coordinate protests against segregation in the city. The protests soon became a mass movement, and Martin Luther King, Jr. arrived in the city to offer his support.

STUDENT ARRESTS

Five black students were arrested on November 22, for holding a sit-in at the lunch counter of a bus terminal in Albany. When the students went to court, the Albany Movement organized a march past the courtrooms and handed in a petition calling for the students to be released. The local newspaper criticized the march, so the Albany Movement responded by boycotting the newspaper and all the businesses that advertised in it. On December 10, a group of Freedom Riders arrived at Albany's train station. The black Freedom Riders entered the whites-only section of the terminal and the white volunteers went into the blacks-only part. They were all arrested. Over the next week, hundreds of students marched in support of the Freedom Riders, and most of them were arrested.

KING COMES TO ALBANY

On December 16, Martin Luther King, Jr., led a march to Albany city hall. All of the marchers, including King, were arrested for marching without permission. While he was in jail, divisions began to appear within the Albany Movement. City leaders promised to desegregate train and bus facilities if the protests stopped. King was released from jail and left Albany. Within a few weeks, it was clear that the city was not going to integrate as the leaders promised, and the city officials also refused to meet leaders of the Albany Movement. King returned to Albany to stand trial. He was sentenced to pay a fine or go to jail. King chose jail, but the fine was paid by an unidentified stranger and King was released.

THE MOVEMENT FAILS

The Albany Movement protests had been going on for nearly a year, and they had not gained any concessions from the city authorities. On July 24, 1962, a demonstration of 2,000 black

Martin Luther King, Jr., led black American protesters down a street in Albany. The 1961 march was just one of the events in the protest against segregation in the city.

Plea to end discrimination

"It is our belief that discrimination based on race, color or religion is fundamentally wrong and contrary to the letter and intent of the Constitution of the United States. It is our aim in the Albany Movement to seek means of ending discriminatory practices in public facilities..."
Letter from the Albany Movement to the Albany City Commission, January 23, 1962.

Albany residents turned violent, and bricks and bottles were thrown at the police. King called for a "Day of Penance" to promote non-violence. The city authorities refused to meet any black leaders until King left town, but when he did leave, the authorities went back on their promise. The Albany Movement had failed.

CROSS-REFERENCE
MARCHES FOR CIVIL RIGHTS: PAGES 22–23, 24–25, 32–33, 38–39

Martin Luther King, Jr. (left), was arrested for marching in Albany.

The Birmingham Campaign

By May 3, 1963, people had been protesting against segregation in Birmingham, Alabama, for over a month. On that day, the Birmingham police chief, Eugene "Bull" Connor, ordered the use of police dogs and high-pressure water hoses to break up protests. This violence brought the Birmingham campaign to national attention and gave the civil rights movement a much-needed victory after the Albany defeat.

AMERICA'S MOST SEGREGATED CITY

Segregation was a part of daily life in Birmingham. Restaurants, buses, and even parks were segregated. "Bull" Connor was a strong believer in segregation and was determined to fight what he saw as interference in Birmingham by outsiders.

PROJECT C

Martin Luther King, Jr., and other members of the Southern Christian Leadership Conference (SCLC) came to Birmingham to fight segregation in the city. They focused their protests against segregation in stores, lunch counters, and public toilets. Their campaign, called Project C, began on April 3, with lunch counter sit-ins. Within two weeks, over 200 people had been arrested. On April 12, King was arrested along with other civil rights leaders.

LETTER FROM BIRMINGHAM JAIL

A day after King's arrest, local white clergymen called for an end to the protests. In jail, King wrote a reply in which he said that the fight against segregation should not be delayed. This was published, and it soon became one of the most important documents in the civil rights movement.

A VIOLENT REACTION

The SCLC called on children in Birmingham to join the protests. On May 2, over 1,000 children ages six to 18 marched through the city singing freedom songs. "Bull" Connor responded by sending 959 children to Birmingham's jails. The next day, the protestors were met with water hoses and police dogs. Television pictures of children being arrested and protestors being attacked by the police were beamed around the world.

THE CAMPAIGN ENDS

Local businesses in Birmingham suffered from the turmoil caused by the protests. They told Burke Marshall,

Teenagers sing freedom songs in Birmingham during a segregation protest march on May 2, 1963.

TIMELINE

THE BIRMINGHAM CAMPAIGN, 1963

April 2, 1963 ▶ Martin Luther King, Jr., and other members of the SCLC discuss their plan against segregation in Birmingham.

April 3, 1963 ▶ Project C begins with peaceful sit-ins at lunch counters.

April 12, 1963 ▶ Martin Luther King, Jr., is arrested.

May 2, 1963 ▶ Schoolchildren march through Birmingham. In response, 959 of the children are jailed.

May 3, 1963 ▶ The Birmingham police chief orders the use of police dogs and high-pressure hoses to break up protests.

May 10, 1963 ▶ Local businesses in Birmingham agree to desegregate.

Firefighters used high-pressure water hoses against demonstrators.

who had been sent to Birmingham by President Kennedy to encourage negotiations, that they would desegregate their businesses. The following night, the Ku Klux Klan held a rally at the city and bombs exploded at the home of King's brother and at the hotel where King was staying. President Kennedy warned the city authorities that he would send in 3,000 troops unless the agreement was honored. Only then did the city mayor honor the agreement.

CROSS-REFERENCE POLICE BRUTALITY: PAGES 32–33, 42–43

The Birmingham problem

"Birmingham is probably the most thoroughly segregated city in the United States. Its ugly record of police brutality is known in every section of this country. Its unjust treatment of Negroes in the courts is a notorious reality. There have been more unsolved bombings of Negro homes and churches in Birmingham than any city in this nation. These are the hard, brutal and unbelievable facts. On the basis of these conditions, Negro leaders sought to negotiate with city fathers. But the political leaders consistently refused to engage in good faith negotiation."
Excerpt from Martin Luther King, Jr., "Letter from Birmingham Jail", April 16, 1963.

The March on Washington

On August 28, 1963, just over 100 years after Lincoln declared slavery was at an end, over 200,000 US citizens came to Washington, DC, to demand fair treatment and equal opportunities for all US citizens. The majority were black, but also many were white.

PLANNING THE MARCH

A. Philip Randolph, a veteran of the civil rights movement, had suggested a march on Washington, DC. It was to highlight unemployment and poverty among black people. However, after the events at Birmingham, Randolph decided to make the march broader in its aims. It was now about ending racial discrimination in the workplace and finally ending segregation throughout the United States.

The main civil rights groups, such as the SCLC, the NAACP, the SNCC, and CORE, were involved in the planning of the march. At first, President Kennedy tried to persuade the leaders to call off the march because of the fear of violence. However, Kennedy backed down and offered the marchers his support.

THE MARCH TAKES PLACE

The march was publicized across the country. From across the nation, Freedom Buses arrived in Washington, DC, and trains were brought in to take people to the city. One group of people walked from New York, and one person even roller-skated from Chicago, about 700 miles (1,145 kilometers) away. By noon on August 28, thousands of placards were held high as marchers walked from the Washington Monument to the Lincoln Memorial. As they waited for the speeches, they listened to folk musicians such as Joan Baez singing "We Shall Overcome."

"I HAVE A DREAM"

The leaders of the march were asked to speak to the crowd for 15 minutes. A. Philip Randolph gave the opening speech. John Lewis, the leader of the

AUGUST 28, 1963

Thousands of demonstrators with placards marched down Constitution Avenue from the Washington Monument to the Lincoln Memorial.

TIMELINE

THE IDEA OF THE MARCH, 1941–1963

June 1941 ▶ A. Philip Randolph first suggests a march through Washington, DC.

1962 ▶ A. Philip Randolph again suggests a march through Washington, DC, as unemployment of black Americans reaches twice that of white Americans.

August 28, 1963 ▶ Over 200,000 people march for civil rights in Washington, DC. Martin Luther King, Jr., gives his "I Have a Dream" speech.

Martin Luther King, Jr., at the Lincoln Memorial on August 28, 1963.

SNCC, gave an angry speech that criticized President Kennedy for not doing more for civil rights. The last speech was by Martin Luther King, Jr. He had a prepared text ready, then the singer Mahalia Jackson shouted out, "Tell them about your dream!" King put aside his prepared text and began his famous "I Have a Dream" speech.

THE MARCH'S IMPACT

The march by itself did not really achieve anything. However, it gave those working for civil rights a greater sense of hope. It also told the people of the United States that the issue of civil rights was not going to go away.

CROSS-REFERENCE MARCHES FOR CIVIL RIGHTS: PAGES 20–21, 22–23, 32–33, 38–39

King's dream

"I have a dream that my four little children will one day live in a nation where they will not be judged by the color of their skin, but by the content of their character."
Excerpt from the speech given by Martin Luther King, Jr., on August 28, 1968.

The Freedom Summer Project

On June 21, 1964, three young volunteers were in Mississippi. They were there as part of a campaign to encourage black people to register to vote. They were arrested for speeding by Cecil Price, a local sheriff, and held for several hours. They were then released and then arrested again by Price. He held on to them until they were taken by members of the Ku Klux Klan to a deserted road, where they were all shot and their bodies buried.

THE COFO

Since late 1961, civil rights groups in the South had led campaigns to show black people how they could register as voters, because fewer than one in five black people of voting age were actually registered to vote. By 1964, over 1.5 million additional black voters had registered to vote. Real progress was being made in every state except one—Mississippi.

In 1962, civil rights groups in Mississippi banded together to form the Council of Federated Organizations (COFO). Their aim was to tackle the problem of the large number of black people who were not registered voters. In late 1963, they decided to launch an ambitious voting rights project for the following summer. It was known as the Freedom Summer Project.

Hundreds of student volunteers were to move into black neighborhoods and encourage registration.

ARRIVAL IN MISSISSIPPI

The first 200 volunteers arrived in Mississippi on Saturday, June 20, and they were immediately met with violence and threats. Along with the three volunteers who were murdered, one other volunteer was killed. Over 1,000 people were arrested, and 37 churches were bombed or burned.

In early August, the bodies of James Chaney, Michael Shwerner, and Andrew Goodman were found, and 21 men were arrested for their murder, but a local court set them free. A year later, seven of the men were found guilty of breaking civil rights laws.

Volunteers for the Freedom Summer Project traveled to Mississippi to inform children and adults about voting, and encourage people to register as voters.

TIMELINE

THE TRAGEDY OF FREEDOM SUMMER, 1963–1965

1963 ▶ COFO launches the Freedom Summer Project for summer 1964 to encourage black people to register to vote.

June 20, 1964 ▶ The first 200 volunteers arrive in Mississippi to violence and threats.

June 21, 1964 ▶ Three volunteers working on the Freedom Summer Project are murdered by the Ku Klux Klan in Mississippi.

August 1964 ▶ The bodies of the volunteers are found, but the state of Mississippi refuses to investigate the murders.

1965 ▶ Seven men are tried and convicted of crimes relating to the murders but spend less than six years in jail.

THE MISSISSIPPI FREEDOM DEMOCRATIC PARTY

The Democratic Party in Mississippi was dominated by white people who were determined to stop black people registering as voters. The COFO reacted by setting up the Mississippi Freedom Democratic Party as a rival to the local Democratic Party. They tried to replace the Democratic Party as the Mississippi representatives at the 1964 National Convention of the national Democratic Party. Although they failed to do this, their presence at the convention did much to highlight the lives of black people in Mississippi.

Martin Luther King, Jr., with photographs of the three civil rights workers murdered in Mississippi in 1964.

CROSS-REFERENCE ENCOURAGING VOTERS: PAGES 28–29, 32–33, 34–35

Register for votes

"I am not here to memorialize James Cheney, I am not here to pay tribute—I am too sick and tired ... I have attended too many memorials, too many funerals ... But the trouble is that you are not sick and tired and for that reason you, yes, you, are to blame ... It's high time that you got angry too, angry enough to go up to the courthouse Monday and register [to vote]—every one of you."

Excerpt of the speech by David Dennis at the memorial for James Cheney, August 7, 1964.

The Civil Rights Act

President Kennedy standing with civil rights and labor leaders, including Martin Luther King, Jr. (second from left).

On July 2, 1964, President Lyndon Johnson signed a new law that had been passed by Congress. The Civil Rights Act outlawed discrimination in voting rights and ended segregation in public places, such as parks, hotels, and restaurants. It also outlawed racial discrimination in the workplace.

PRESIDENT KENNEDY

It was President John F. Kennedy who first proposed a Civil Rights Act in June 1963. He wanted the act to completely outlaw segregation throughout the United States and to get rid of racially based barriers to employment or membership in a labor union. Members of Congress from the Southern states tried to delay the bill. However, the march on Washington in August 1963 encouraged the supporters of the bill in both the country and in Congress.

"LET US CONTINUE"

On November 22, 1963, President Kennedy was assassinated in Dallas, Texas. The news of his death was greeted with cheers and applause in some parts of the South, where many regarded Kennedy as a Northern liberal who did not appear to be on their side.

Civil rights leaders mourned Kennedy's death and worried what this might do to the Civil Rights Act. One of the reasons for their worries was that Vice President Johnson now became president of the United States. Johnson came from Texas, a Southern state, and was regarded as being more conservative than Kennedy. He had voted against earlier Civil Rights Acts and had weakened the Civil Rights Act of 1957. However, in his first address to Congress, he made it clear that he would continue with the bill and that he had no intention of changing any part of the act.

Main points of the act

- It outlawed racial segregation in schools, public places, and employment.
- Discrimination in the workplace because of color, race, religion, sex, or nationality was prohibited.
- Employers had to treat all employees equally regardless of color, race, religion, sex, or nationality.

GETTING THROUGH CONGRESS

President Johnson held several private meetings with members of Congress, particularly those from the South, and warned them that there was not going to be any compromise on the bill. They either had to accept all of the bill or reject it completely. Many of the Southern congressmen did not want to be seen as wreckers of the bill, and several saw that public opinion throughout the country demanded the bill be passed. On June 19, the act was passed by Congress, and on July 2, President Johnson signed the bill into law.

CROSS-REFERENCE
THE FIRST CIVIL RIGHTS ACT: PAGES 4–5

President Johnson signed the Civil Rights Act, 1964, in the presence of civil rights leaders, government officials, and the press.

The Death of Malcolm X

On February 21, 1965, black civil rights leader Malcolm X began to speak to a packed hall in New York. There was a disturbance in the crowd, and a man ran forward and shot him in the chest with a shotgun. Two other men then started firing at Malcolm X with handguns. He was hit 16 times. One of the most charismatic and controversial figures in the civil rights movement was dead.

THE NATION OF ISLAM

When Malcolm X (born Malcolm Little) was a young man in the 1940s, he drifted between cities and quickly moved from job to job. In January 1946, he was arrested for burglary and was sentenced to eight years in prison. While he was in prison, he became a Muslim and joined the Nation of Islam. On his release from prison in 1952, Malcolm X worked with Elijah Muhammad, the leader of the Nation of Islam, and he soon became known as a fiery speaker who inspired many black Americans, especially in the Northern states. As a member of the Nation of Islam, he believed that black people were superior to white people. Malcolm X advocated the complete separation of black and white people.

Malcolm X was a fierce critic of many civil rights leaders, who he thought were simply being used by white people. He did not believe in non-violence and instead said that

FEBRUARY 21, 1965

Martin Luther King, Jr., and Malcolm X at their only meeting, in the halls of the US Capitol, observing the signing of the Voting Rights Act.

black people should use any means to defend themselves.

LEAVING THE NATION OF ISLAM

In March 1964, Malcolm X left the Nation of Islam after increasing disagreements with Elijah Muhammad. He believed that the Nation of Islam's religious teachings were too rigid and not political enough. He founded the Organization of Afro-American Unity (OAAU), which was dedicated to finding ways to link black people around the world. After a pilgrimage to Mecca, he abandoned his belief in the inferiority of white people and, on his return to the United States, started to find ways of working with some civil rights leaders. He also became a popular speaker at colleges and universities around the country.

THE RISE AND FALL OF A LEADER, 1946–1965

January 1946 ▶ Malcolm X is arrested for burglary and spends eight years in prison.

1952 ▶ On release from prison, Malcolm X works with Elijah Muhammad, the leader of the Nation of Islam.

March 1964 ▶ Malcolm X leaves the Nation of Islam and founds the OAAU.

February 21, 1965 ▶ Malcolm X is shot dead in New York.

DANGEROUS ENEMIES

Leaving the Nation of Islam meant that Malcolm X had made many dangerous enemies. There were several attempts to kill him by members of the Nation of Islam. It was three members of this organization who killed him in New York.

CROSS-REFERENCE
ASSASSINATIONS:
PAGES 38–39

Being American

"Sitting at the table doesn't make you a diner, unless you eat some of what's on that plate. Being here in America doesn't make you an American. Being born here in America doesn't make you an American. Why, if birth made you American, you wouldn't need any legislation; you wouldn't need any amendments to the Constitution; you wouldn't be faced with civil rights filibustering in Washington, DC, right now."

Malcolm X's "The Ballot or the Bullet" speech, April 3, 1964.

Two policemen carry a stretcher bearing civil rights leader Malcom X after he was shot by an assassin at a hall in New York while giving a speech.

The March at Selma

SNCC leader John Lewis (light coat, center) was beaten by state troops during the attempted march from Selma to Montgomery on March 7. Lewis was later admitted to the hospital with a possible skull fracture.

On March 7, 1965, 600 local civil rights supporters in Selma, Alabama, gathered to march to Montgomery, the state capital of Alabama. The marchers intended to ask Governor George Wallace to protect black people as they registered as voters. The marchers had reached the Edmund Pettus Bridge in Selma when they were attacked by local police and troops with tear gas, whips, and clubs.

"WE ARE DEMANDING THE BALLOT"

In 1964, only 23 percent of black people of voting age in Alabama were registered to vote. In Selma, attempts to encourage black people to register were met with resistance. The local sheriff, Jim Clark, arrested the Student Nonviolent Coordinating Committee (SNCC) volunteers who came to help with the registration process. Voter registration was only allowed two days a month, and black people who tried to register often had their registrations rejected.

In January 1965, Martin Luther King, Jr., announced in Selma that black people were not asking, but demanding, the right to vote. King and several SNCC volunteers led several marches in Selma in an attempt to get more black people on the voting rolls. By the end of February, nearly 3,000 people, including King, had been arrested. Malcolm X came to Selma and told a crowd in a local church that he supported the work that King was doing. On the same day, President Johnson held a press conference in which he supported the voter registration drive in Selma.

THE THREE MARCHES

The attacks on the black marchers on March 7, were televised. Pictures of people fleeing from tear gas and police officers charging on horseback toward the marchers led to members of Congress and President Johnson condemning the violence. King announced that another march would

TIMELINE	**SELMA TO MONTGOMERY, 1964–1965**
1964	▶ Only 23 percent of black people of voting age in Alabama are registered to vote.
January 1965	▶ Martin Luther King, Jr., and SNCC volunteers march in Selma to encourage black people to register to vote.
February 1965	▶ Nearly 3,000 people, including King, are arrested.
March 7, 1965	▶ The first march from Selma to Montgomery reaches the Edmund Pettus Bridge, where the marchers are attacked by police and troops.
March 9, 1965	▶ The second march from Selma to Montgomery turns back when the path is blocked.
March 21, 1965	▶ The third march from Selma toMontgomery begins. The marchers arrive four days later.

take place on March 9. The marchers crossed the bridge and were stopped on the road to Montgomery. King decided not to proceed and led the marchers back to Selma. On March 21, the third march from Selma to Montgomery began. This time there were no police officers to stop them. Led by King, over 5,000 people started the march at Selma and headed toward Montgomery. Four days later, they arrived, with the number of marchers at over 30,000. King gave a speech to the crowd telling them that they did not have long to wait for justice to finally arrive.

Martin Luther King, Jr., and his wife, Coretta, led a five-day march to the Alabama state capital of Montgomery on March 25, 1965.

CROSS-REFERENCE ENCOURAGING VOTERS: PAGES 26–27, 28–29, 34–35

No respect for democracy

"I am shocked at the terrible reign of terror that took place in Alabama today. Negro citizens engaged in a peaceful and orderly march to protest racial injustice were beaten, brutalized and harassed by state troopers, and Alabama revealed its law enforcement agents have no respect for democracy nor the rights of its Negro citizens."
Martin Luther King, Jr., in a press statement to the *New York Times*, March 7, 1965.

The Voting Rights Act

AUGUST 6, 1965

On August 6, 1965, President Johnson signed into law the Voting Rights Act. The act enforced the 15th Amendment, which stated that a US citizen could not be denied the right to vote because of his or her race. The act also outlawed any barriers to voter registration.

THE ATTACK AT SELMA

President Johnson was greatly moved by the attacks on the Selma marchers on March 7. He held a press conference in which he said that every US citizen had the right to register as a voter. He promised that he would find a way to give that right to every person.

On March 15, less than a week before the third Selma to Montgomery march, President Johnson announced that he would be sending a voting rights bill to Congress that would "strike down all restrictions used to deny the people the right to vote."

That evening, President Johnson delivered a televised address to Congress in which he asked Congress to pass his voting rights bill. He mentioned the Selma protest several times and even called it a turning point in US history.

President Johnson signed the Voting Rights Act on August 6, 1965.

THE BILL IS PASSED

Although there was some resistance to the bill, it passed easily in Congress on August 3 and 4. For the signing ceremony due to take place on August 6, President Johnson invited several major civil rights leaders, such as Martin Luther King, Jr., James Farmer, and Roy Wilkins. He also invited Rosa Parks, who had started the Montgomery bus boycott, and Vivien Malone, who could only go to the University of Alabama in 1963 when she was accompanied by troops.

The signing ceremony took place in the President's Room of the Capitol building. It was the same room where President Lincoln had

March 15, 1965	President Johnson announces that he will send a new voting rights bill to Congress.
August 3–4 1965	The Voting Rights Act is passed by Congress.
August 6 1965	President Johnson signs the Voting Rights Act into law.
November 1966	Edward Brooke is elected to the Senate and becomes the first black person in the Senate since 1881.

Main points of the act

• It outlawed any voting qualifications.
• States could not change voting rules without government approval.
• It became illegal to stop a person from voting if they did not speak English.

signed the Emancipation Proclamation 104 years earlier.

PASSED AGAIN

There are various parts of the Voting Rights Act that have to be periodically renewed by Congress and signed by the president. These parts were renewed in 1970, 1975, 1982, and 2006. In 2006, President George W. Bush signed the Voting Rights Act in the presence of Jesse Jackson, Rosa Parks, and members of Martin Luther King, Jr.'s, family.

**CROSS-REFERENCE
ENCOURAGING
VOTERS: PAGES
26–27, 28–29,
32–33**

In 1966, the first black Americans cast votes under the new Voting Rights Act.

Stokely Carmichael and Black Power

On June 7, 1966, the leader of the Student Nonviolent Coordinating Committee (SNCC), Stokely Carmichael, joined a march with other civil rights leaders. Some of the younger leaders were beginning to question how effective non-violence really was. They also objected to the presence of white supporters on the march. Carmichael first used the phrase "black power" during this march.

STOKELY CARMICHAEL

Carmichael became chairman of the SNCC in 1966. Under his leadership, the SNCC began to move towards a more radical position and took up the slogan "black power." For Carmichael, this meant that black Americans should take control of their own communities. It also meant that complete non-violence was rejected and that if black people encountered violence, then they were entitled to use violence in return. Carmichael also wanted black people to be prouder of their color and to learn more about the history and culture of black people.

THE BLACK PANTHER PARTY

Inspired by Stokely Carmichael and the speeches of Malcolm X, new black nationalist groups formed among young black people in the cities of the Northern states of the

Stokely Carmichael was active in the 1960s civil rights movement and traveled around the world to promote his theories. Here, he is speaking in London, UK.

country. In October 1966, Huey Newton and Bobby Seale, two young men who were working in a community center in Oakland, California, founded the Black Panther Party for Self-Defense.

The chief goal of the Black Panther Party was to protect the black residents of Oakland from what was seen as police brutality. The party also started various programs to help Oakland's poor black residents.

The Black Panthers remained a small group, but they got a lot of media attention because they dressed in military uniforms and openly carried guns. Hostility between the Black

Panthers and the local police led to several shootings between them.

THE DECLINE OF THE BLACK PANTHERS

In the late 1960s, the Black Panthers began to drop some of their demands for black control of their own affairs. They started to work more closely with white revolutionary groups as they became more involved in planning for a violent revolution. This brought the Black Panthers into conflict with other radical black groups. In 1967, the FBI began to infiltrate the Black Panthers and weakened them from the inside. The party eventually fell apart in the mid-1970s, but the idea of black power became an important part of the civil rights movement.

US athletes give the black power salute on the winners' podium at the Mexico Olympic Games, 1968.

**CROSS-REFERENCE
THE SNCC:
PAGES 16–17,
18–19, 32–33**

The black panther

"I would like to let the people here tonight know why we chose this black panther as our emblem. Many people have been asking this question for a long time ... This black panther is a vicious animal, as you know. He never bothers anyone, but when you start pushing him, he moves backwards, backwards, and backwards into his corner, and then he comes out to destroy everything that's before him."
Speech by John Hulett, a leading member of the Black Panthers, 1966.

The Death of Martin Luther King, Jr.

Martin Luther King, Jr., was shot on the balcony of the Lorraine Motel. Here, he lies on the balcony floor while people around him point in the direction of the gunshots.

On April 4, 1968, Martin Luther King, Jr., was in Memphis, Tennessee. He was there to help a group of black sanitation workers fight for better wages and working conditions. King was standing on the balcony of the Lorraine Motel when a single shot rang out. King was hit in the head, and an hour later, he was declared dead. His killer, James Earl Ray, was arrested two months later.

A NEW DIRECTION

After the successes of the Civil Rights Act and the Voting Rights Act, Martin Luther King, Jr., was looking for a new direction for the civil rights movement. He was also concerned about the rise of the black power movement, particularly because it rejected non-violence. In March 1968,

he was asked by striking black sanitation workers in Memphis for help. They felt that they were being unfairly treated compared to the white sanitation workers in the city. The mayor of Memphis refused to meet the workers and threatened to fire them if they did not return to work.

On March 28, King led a march to city hall. The march was attacked by local police, and several marchers fought back. This turned into a riot. By the time the riot had finished, over 150 stores were burned or looted, 60 people were injured, and a 16-year-old had been killed. On April 3, King attended a rally of 2,000 people in which he spoke about his own death.

A VIOLENT END

Within hours of King's death becoming public news, there were riots in Chicago, Detroit, Boston, and Washington, DC. There were also smaller incidents of violence in 130 other cities. Black leaders called for calm and asked people to express their anger in a non-violent way. Stokely Carmichael called for black people to carry guns to defend themselves. By the end of the week, 46 people were dead and over 3,000 people were injured.

MARTIN LUTHER KING DAY

On November 2, 1983, President Ronald Reagan signed a bill that made the third Monday of every January Martin Luther King Day. This is only one of three federal holidays to commemorate individuals (the others are Christopher Columbus and George Washington). It was first observed in 1986 and is now celebrated in all 50 states.

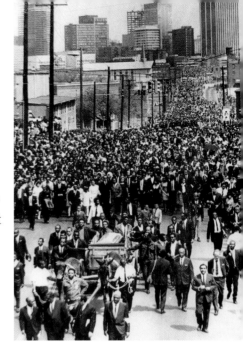

The funeral procession of over 100,000 mourners behind the coffin of Martin Luther King, Jr., in Atlanta, Georgia.

CROSS-REFERENCE ASSASSINATIONS: PAGES 30–31

No more violence

"We can move in that direction as a country, in greater polarization—black people amongst blacks, and white amongst whites, filled with hatred toward one another. Or we can make an effort, as Martin Luther King did, to understand, and to comprehend, and replace that violence, that stain of bloodshed that has spread across our land, with an effort to understand, compassion, and love."

Speech by Robert Kennedy on the day of King's assassination.

Jesse Jackson

Jesse Jackson (second left) with Martin Luther King, Jr. (second right), on the day before King's assassination.

On March 8, 1988, Jesse Jackson became the first black American with a realistic chance of becoming the Democratic Party candidate for the 1988 presidential election. He won the support of seven states. However, he failed to get the support of some of the larger states, and Michael Dukakis became the Democratic candidate.

A CIVIL RIGHTS WORKER

In 1965, the young Jesse Jackson took part in the Selma to Montgomery march. As a result of this, he became deeply involved in the civil rights movement. Martin Luther King, Jr., put him in charge of Operation Breadbasket, which organized boycotts of businesses that discriminated against black people. He was also present at the motel when King was shot. Later, through the organization People United to Save Humanity (PUSH), Jackson continued to champion the rights of black workers and to provide educational opportunities for young black people.

RUNNING FOR PRESIDENT

In November 1983, Jackson announced his campaign to become the Democratic candidate for the 1984 presidential election. He was dismissed by many as a minor candidate with no chance of winning the Democratic nomination. He surprised everybody by coming in third, with 18 percent of Democrats choosing him as their preferred candidate. He did well by appealing to various groups, such as Hispanics, Native Americans, and black Americans, that had been ignored by the other candidates.

PUSH

PUSH was founded by Jesse Jackson in 1971 to try to help black people to help themselves. In the 1970s, PUSH worked with black workers, homeowners, and business leaders and encouraged young black people to continue in education through reading schemes and scholarships. PUSH also encouraged large companies to employ more black people.

TIMELINE

JESSE JACKSON, 1965–1988

March 1965 ▶ Jackson takes part in the Selma to Mongomery march.

November 1983 ▶ Jackson announces that he's running to be the Democratic candidate in the 1984 presidential election.

1984 ▶ Jackson forms the National Rainbow Coalition.

March 8, 1988 ▶ Jackson runs again to be the Democratic candidate in the 1988 presidential election.

Four years later, he tried again. This time he did much better and was briefly the front-runner to become the Democratic candidate for the 1988 presidential election. It was felt by many people that he was the victim of the so-called Bradley effect in Wisconsin. This is when white people say that they will vote for a black candidate but then vote for a white candidate on the day of an election.

Jesse Jackson speaks to supporters at the Democratic National Convention in 1988. Thousands turned out to support him.

THE RAINBOW COALITION

After the 1984 presidential elections, Jesse Jackson formed the National Rainbow Coalition. This was intended to bring together groups of people that Jackson believed had been neglected by President Reagan, such as black Americans, small farmers, people with disabilities, Native Americans, and labor union members. The purpose of the Rainbow Coalition was to give each of these groups more of a say in government. It later merged with PUSH.

CROSS-REFERENCE PRESIDENTIAL ELECTIONS: PAGES 44–45

The Los Angeles Race Riots

On April 29, 1992, Los Angeles saw the start of the largest race riots in American history. They lasted for three days and only came to an end when President George H. W. Bush sent in troops to restore order.

THE BEATING OF RODNEY KING

On March 3, 1991, a young black American named Rodney King was stopped in his car by officers from the Los Angeles Police Department (LAPD). The four officers started to beat King with their batons and then kick him when he fell to the ground. The whole incident was caught on videotape and was broadcast around the world. It increased tensions between black people and the police in Los Angeles.

The four police officers who were seen on the videotape appeared in court. The case was heard in a wealthy part of California, Ventura County. The jury that heard the case was made up of 10 white people, one Hispanic, and one Asian. The jury found three of the officers innocent and said that there was not enough evidence to find the fourth officer guilty.

THE LOS ANGELES RIOTS

Almost immediately after the jury had decided the fate of the four police officers, thousands of angry people took to the streets of Los Angeles.

For three days, stores and businesses were burned and looted, and several white and Hispanic people were attacked by angry mobs. President Bush, while sympathizing over the Rodney King case, said that he could not allow violence on the streets of Los Angeles.

A video clip showed the beating of Rodney King by Los Angeles police officers. Despite this evidence, the four officers were found innocent by members of the jury.

"Let's get along"

"People, I just want to say, can we all just get along? Can we stop making it horrible? We're all stuck here for a while. Let's try to work it out."
Rodney King tries to halt the riots sparked by the acquittal of the police officers accused of beating him, 1992.

Fires raged in Los Angeles, set off in the riots after Los Angeles police officers were acquitted of beating Rodney King.

On the third day, King himself appealed for calm to return to Los Angeles. This, along with the arrival of thousands of troops, meant that normality began to return. By the end of the riots, over 50 people were dead and thousands were injured.

THE CHRISTOPHER COMMISSION

In the aftermath of the riots, the mayor of Los Angeles, Tom Bradley, asked Warren Christopher to investigate the LAPD and find out why the Rodney King case happened. Christopher found that police officers regularly used much more force than they were supposed to. He also discovered that racism was still a problem among some

CROSS-REFERENCE POLICE BRUTALITY: PAGES 22–23, 32–33

The Election of Barack Obama

On January 20, 2009, Barack Obama was sworn in as the 44th president of the United States on the West Front of the Capitol in Washington, DC.

On January 20, 2009, Barack Obama was sworn in as the 44th president of the United States. He is also the first black US president. For many, his election to the highest office in the United States was the culmination of all of the struggles of the civil rights movement in the 1950s and 1960s.

EARLY LIFE

Barack Obama was born in 1961 to a Kenyan father and a white American mother, spending much of his childhood in Hawaii and Indonesia. He studied law at Harvard University and became the first black president of the *Harvard Law Review*. He later went to Chicago, where he worked as a lawyer dealing in civil rights cases among poorer black communities. He also taught at the University of Chicago. From 1997 until 2003, Obama was a state senator in Illinois. In 2004, he was elected to the US Senate, becoming the only black American in the Senate.

BECOMING PRESIDENT

Just three years later, Obama announced his intention to run as Democratic candidate for the 2008 presidential elections. Like Jesse Jackson before him, many felt that he had little chance of winning. However, by the end of 2007, it was a contest between Obama and Hillary Clinton—a black man and a woman. In the end, he won the nomination and went forward to become the Democratic Party's presidential candidate. There were some people who thought that the Bradley effect that had affected Jesse Jackson's 1988 campaign might also hurt Obama's chances. However, in November 2008, Barack Obama won the presidential election.

TIMELINE

THE PATH TO THE PRESIDENCY, 1997–2009

1997–2003 ▶ Obama is a state senator in Illinois.

2004 ▶ Obama is elected to be a member of the US Senate and becomes the first black American in the Senate.

2006 ▶ Obama announces that he will run for president.

2007 ▶ Obama becomes the Democratic candidate for the presidential election.

November 2008 ▶ Obama wins the presidential election.

January 20, 2009 ▶ Barack Obama becomes the 44th president of the United States.

Barack Obama delivering his victory speech after winning the presidential election.

OBAMA AND RACE

During the election campaign, Barack Obama brought up the issue of race only once. On March 18, 2008 in Philadelphia, he spoke about his own mixed racial identity. He said that he understood white people who resented affirmative action programs that seemed to favor black people. He also pointed out the continued discrimination against black people in many areas of life. His speech ended by asking citizens to put aside their suspicions of each other and work for a common good.

CROSS-REFERENCE PRESIDENTIAL ELECTIONS: PAGES 40–41

A day to remember

"This election had many firsts and many stories that will be told for generations. But one that's on my mind tonight is about a woman who cast her ballot in Atlanta ... Ann Nixon Cooper is 106 years old. She was born just a generation past slavery ... when someone like her couldn't vote for two reasons—because she was a woman and because of the color of her skin ... She was there for the buses in Montgomery, the hoses in Birmingham, a bridge in Selma, and a preacher from Atlanta who told a people that 'We shall overcome.' Yes we can."

Barack Obama's victory speech on the night that he won the 2008 presidential election.

Key Figures of Civil Rights

STOKELY CARMICHAEL (1941–1998), CIVIL RIGHTS LEADER, CHAIRMAN OF THE SNCC

Born in Trinidad and Tobago, Stokely Carmichael moved to the United States when he was two years old. He was introduced to the Student Nonviolent Coordinating Committee (SNCC) when he was at Howard University in the 1960s, and he took part in the Freedom Summer Project and helped to organize the Mississippi Freedom Democratic Party. In 1966, he became chairman of the SNCC and coined the term "black power." In 1967, he stepped down as chairman and joined the Black Panther Party, which was against non-violence. He died of cancer in New York in 1998.

WILLIAM DuBOIS (1868–1963), CIVIL RIGHTS LEADER

William DuBois was born in Massachusetts to a black mother and a father of mixed race. He earned a degree from Fisk University in Nashville, Tennessee, and also attended Harvard College and the University of Berlin. He became the first black American with a PhD from Harvard University. William DuBois became one of the most prominent civil rights leaders of the first half of the 20th century, tirelessly working to improve the lives of black Americans.

JOHN LEWIS (1940–), CIVIL RIGHTS LEADER, CHAIRMAN OF THE SNCC

Born in Troy, Alabama, John Lewis attended the American Baptist College and Fisk University in Nashville, Tennessee, where he took part in sit-in protests. He was beaten by a mob as a Freedom Rider in 1961. As chairman of the SNCC, he spoke at the march on Washington in 1963. In 1965, he was beaten by police in the first Selma to Montgomery march. He left the SNCC in 1966 and worked with community organizations. In 1986, John Lewis became a congressman for Georgia. He is a member of the US House of Representatives.

MARTIN LUTHER KING, JR. (1929–1968), CIVIL RIGHTS LEADER, PRESIDENT OF THE SCLC

This pastor born in Atlanta and practicing in Alabama became one of the most important leaders of the civil rights movement. He organized the Montgomery bus boycott in 1955, was a founder and president of the Southern Christian Leadership Conference (SCLC) in 1957, took major parts in the Albany Movement in 1961 and the Birmingham Campaign in 1963, and led the march on Washington that same year. In 1964, Martin Luther King, Jr., became the youngest man to receive the Nobel Peace Prize. On April 4, 1968, King was assassinated at the Lorraine Motel in Memphis.

MALCOLM X (1925–1965), CIVIL RIGHTS LEADER

Born in Omaha, Nebraska, as Malcolm Little, Malcolm X had a difficult childhood. By the time he was 13, his father had died and his mother had been committed to a mental institution. He became involved in crime and, in 1945, was sentenced to eight years in prison, where he joined the Nation of Islam. After leaving prison, he became a leader of this organization for almost 12 years. However, tension between him and Elijah Muhammad, the head of the Nation of Islam, caused him to leave. Less than a year later, Malcolm X was assassinated by members of the Nation of Islam while speaking in New York.

ROSA PARKS (1913–2005), CIVIL RIGHTS ACTIVIST

Rosa Parks was born in Alabama and grew up in Montgomery, where she cared for her mother and grandmother. She married in 1932, and her husband was a member of the National Association for the Advancement of Colored People (NAACP). In 1943, Parks became secretary to the president of the NAACP. In 1955, she refused to obey segregation laws on a bus and was arrested. She helped to organize the successful Montgomery bus boycott with civil rights leaders and became a civil rights icon but afterward found it difficult to find work. She died on October 24, 2005 at the age of 92.

A. PHILIP RANDOLPH (1889–1979), CIVIL RIGHTS LEADER

Born in Florida, the son of a minister, Asa Philip Randolph studied economics and philosophy at New York City College. In 1917, he founded *The Messenger*, a magazine that campaigned for black civil rights. In the 1930s, he founded the first successful black trade union. During World War II, A. Philip Randolph campaigned for racial equality in the military, which resulted in the US government banning segregation in the armed forces in July 1948. After first suggesting a march on Washington in 1941, A. Philip Randolph finally helped to organize the successful march in 1963. He continued to campaign for black workers in his later years. He died in New York on May 16, 1979.

MOORFIELD STOREY (1845–1929), CIVIL RIGHTS LEADER, FIRST PRESIDENT OF THE NAACP

Moorfield Storey was born in Roxbury, Massachusetts. He graduated from Harvard in 1866 and became a lawyer in 1869, moving on to found a law practice in Boston and be the president of the American Bar Association in 1896. He championed civil rights for black Americans, Native Americans, and immigrants, and became the first president of the NAACP. As a lawyer, he fought against segregation laws and won key cases for civil rights.

Glossary

activist person who actively supports something

amendment change or addition to something

appeal when a court case is taken to a higher court to be heard again

assassination the killing of a public figure

bayonet knife that fits in the muzzle of a gun

boycott refuse to use something

campaign series of operations pursued to accomplish a specific purpose

concession backing down on a point

Congress lawmaking part of the US government, comprising the Senate and the House of Representatives

Constitution set of laws followed by people in the United States

cooperation working together

desegregate to stop keeping black and white people apart

discriminate to treat one group of people in a worse way than other groups

escort someone who accompanies and protects another person

FBI Federal Bureau of Investigation—an agency of the US Department of Justice

integrate bring everyone together

Jim Crow laws laws supporting the segregation of black and white people, named after a black character in a minstrel show

jury a group of people who are chosen at random to come together and give a verdict on a case in a court of law

Ku Klux Klan society of racist white people that terrorized and killed black people in the South with the aim of keeping black people in an inferior position

labor union also called trade union—an organization of workers linked by a common aim, usually to improve working conditions

legislation laws created by government

lynch murder, usually carried out by an angry mob of people

mass movement being supported by large sections of society

National Guardsmen US military troops that help during emergencies

negotiations to discuss arguments and come to a mutual understanding

petition a request to change something, usually given to a government

pilgrimage journey to a sacred place or shrine

placards signs or sign-like objects for display in public

poverty state of being poor and not necessarily having the means to live

privileges certain rights, for example given by a government

racial discrimination treating people badly because they belong to a particular racial group

racism treating individuals or groups differently because they belong to a different race

radical in favor of revolutionary changes in current conditions, organizations, or institutions

rally to come together for a common purpose

rights entitlements, usually governed by law, that aim to protect an individual and help life to be lived without discrimination or repression

riot wild, unlawful, sometimes violent disturbance caused by many people

secession process of withdrawing from something

segregation keeping black and white people apart

sit-ins means of peaceful protests first used by civil rights protestors in 1960, when they sat down in restaurants, disobeying segregation regulations, and refused to leave

slavery ownership of other human beings (slaves)

Supreme Court top legal institution in the United States

tear gas gas that irritates the eyes and causes blinding tears

trial when parties come together to discuss two sides of a dispute in a court of law

unconstitutional not in agreement with the US Constitution

veteran person who has much experience or is practiced in an activity

Further Information

BOOKS

FOR CHILDREN

Kellaher, Karen and the Editors of *Time for Kids*. *Rosa Parks: Civil Rights Pioneer*. Collins, 2007.

Ritchie, Nigel. *The Civil Rights Movement*. Wayland, 2002.

Sanders, Vivienne. *Civil Rights in the USA 1945–68*. Hodder Murray, 2008.

Shuster, Karen, Neil Morris, Andrew Langley, and John Meany. *Was the Civil Rights Movement Successful?* Heinemann, 2008.

FOR OLDER READERS AND TEACHERS

Bates, Daisy. *The Long Shadow of Little Rock*. University of Arkansas Press, 2007.

Kirk, John A. *Martin Luther King Jr. and the Civil Rights Movement*. Palgrave Macmillan, 2007.

Oates, Stephen B. *Let the Trumpet Sound: A Life of Martin Luther King, Jr.* Harper, 1994.

DVDs

Dr. Martin Luther King, A Historical Perspective A documentary that uses rare film footage and photographs to chronicle the civil rights movement. Detal Home Entertainment, 2005.

Malcolm X A biographical film. Pathe Distribution, 2001.

WEBSITES

www.nypl.org/research/sc/sc.html The Schomburg Center for Research in Black Culture

www.usconstitution.net/dream.html The whole text of Martin Luther King, Jr.'s "I Have a Dream" speech

http://nmaahc.si.edu/ The Smithsonian National Museum of African American History

www.naacp.org/ The NAACP website

www.loc.gov/rr/program/bib/civilrights/home.html The Library of Congress civil rights resource

www.crmvet.org/ Images and stories of the civil rights movement in the 1960s

Index

Numbers in **bold** refer to photographs.